FOR:

. . . .

. . . .

Town&Country

WEDDING
SPEECHES
& TOASTS

CAROLINE TIGER

HEARST BOOKS
A division of Sterling Publishing Co., Inc.

New York / London
www.sterlingpublishing.com

Copyright © 2008 by Sterling Publishing Co., Inc.

All rights reserved.

Library of Congress Cataloging-in-Publication Data
Tiger, Caroline.
  Town & country : wedding speeches & toasts / Caroline Tiger.
      p. cm.
  Includes bibliographical references and index.
  ISBN-13: 978-1-58816-622-7 (alk. paper)
  ISBN-10: 1-58816-622-8 (alk. paper)
  1. Wedding etiquette. 2. Weddings—Planning. I. Title.
  BJ2051.T54 2007
  395.2'2—dc22

                                    2006038695

10 9 8 7 6 5 4 3 2 1

Book design by Barbara Balch
Illustrations by Ann Boyajian

Published by Hearst Books
A Division of Sterling Publishing Co., Inc.
387 Park Avenue South, New York, NY 10016

*Town & Country and Hearst Books are trademarks
of Hearst Communications, Inc.*

www.townandcountrymag.com

For information about custom editions, special sales, premium and
corporate purchases, please contact Sterling Special Sales Department
at 800-805-5489 or specialsales@sterlingpub.com.

Distributed in Canada by Sterling Publishing
C/o Canadian Manda Group, 165 Dufferin Street
Toronto, Ontario, Canada M6K 3H6

Distributed in Australia by Capricorn Link (Australia) Pty. Ltd.
P.O. Box 704, Windsor, NSW 2756 Australia

Manufactured in China

Sterling ISBN 13: 978-1-58816-622-7
        ISBN 10: 1-58816-622-8

CONTENTS

FOREWORD

THERE ARE PRECIOUS FEW OCCURRENCES left today that require certain forms of protocol. A wedding is one of them. In our e-mail–mad world, we've become careless (or been allowed to) about what we say and how we say it. Spelling mistakes, commonly made, are instantly forgiven. Informal shorthand ("cu2nite") is widely used, and proper punctuation is deemed unimportant. So it is, too, with behavior. Breaches of conduct are not unusual, nor are they considered all that offensive. Indeed when we meet someone, whether a child or an adult, who demonstrates exquisite manners, we are more often than not totally amazed. A dismal situation.

Weddings, however, seem to bring out the best in us. We dress better, act better and observe what rules remain—all in honor of the bride and groom and their respective families. This doesn't apply to everyone, of course. There will always be the exception, who sees no

> *MARRIAGE IS THE MOST*
> *NATURAL STATE OF MAN,*
> *AND THE STATE IN WHICH*
> *YOU WILL FIND SOLID HAPPINESS.*
> —BENJAMIN FRANKLIN

problem in arriving late, wearing unsuitable attire and calling attention to himself for all the wrong reasons.

It is not just the wedding day itself that involves adhering to long-held traditions; there are events leading up to it that require a certain amount of finesse (the engagement party and the bridal shower, for example), and there are roles that members of the wedding—not just the bride and groom—are expected to play.

This book is intended as a guide for just those situations. Whether you are the mother of the bride, a groomsman or the maid of honor, what you do and say will be relevant to the occasion. While the rules for wedding behavior have loosened considerably in the past fifty years, they haven't vanished altogether. Hurray, we say.

We at *Town & Country* strongly suggest you pay attention to the advice you will find within these pages. For one thing, it will ease you into the spirit of the event.

For another, it will help you do your part to pave the way to the Big Day for all those involved.

We've tried to provide for every eventuality, although we may have inadvertently missed a few. We didn't, for instance, address what to wear at an eco-wedding, although it's probably safe to say that fur jackets or polyester would not be welcome. Nor did we explore the role of extended families, such as ex-spouses, out-of-favor siblings and distant cousins who are offended not to have received an invitation. But we pretty much cover everything else. Thanks for that thoroughness goes to our author, Caroline Tiger.

In addition to the advice, we've also included a section on weddings toasts and how to deliver one with confidence and charm.

There are many good ones here—even a few funny ones (George Jessel's "Marriage is a mistake every man should make."). Feel free to borrow from the selection. In the end, however, the toast maker may want to create one of his or her own—and those, invariably, are the most moving and heartfelt. Just remember these three words: don't wing it.

Pamela Fiori, Editor in Chief,
Town & Country

INTRODUCTION

THERE'S NO QUESTION AS TO WHAT TO SAY when your dear friend or your son or daughter announces his or her engagement. "Congratulations!" you'll exclaim. Or "Great news. I'm so happy for you!" After reveling in the first blush of excitement, you may be left wondering "Now what?" Though weddings at their most fundamental haven't changed much in the past century, each individual celebration manages to be completely new and different. There are recent across-the-board adaptations: save-the-date cards are a relatively new phenomenon, a response to a culture that's increasingly overscheduled. And today's brides are the self-appointed CEOs of their own enterprises, whereas a generation ago, the mothers of the brides were often in charge. But what ultimately flavors a wedding is the bride and groom's unique vision. Is it a formal couple planning a black-tie affair in a cosmopolitan venue? Or is the couple planning a rustic, quietly elegant reception in a charming countryside villa? Most important: how do you fit into this vision? Which brings us back to the pregnant pause after that first "Congratulations."

Either from experience or by osmosis you've picked up on the fact that parents and attendants of brides and grooms play integral roles leading up to and during the wedding. Just as you're a key player in your friend or child's life, so you'll remain throughout their wedding journey. You know that you'll be responsible for planning parties, buying gifts, accompanying the bride on dress fittings and writing a toast, but how do you go about executing the details? This book is meant to transform that thorny thicket into a clearcut path.

> *THERE IS NO MORE LOVELY, FRIENDLY*
> *AND CHARMING RELATIONSHIP,*
> *COMMUNION OR COMPANY*
> *THAN A GOOD MARRIAGE.*
> —*MARTIN LUTHER*

A Few Words on Etiquette

THE ADVICE IN THESE PAGES nods first and foremost to tradition and so-called old-fashioned etiquette for several reasons. A wedding involves two families coming together, and within those families there are guaranteed to be many different personalities and long-standing and possibly different ways of communicating. Treading lightly and squarely along a prescribed path is one way to avoid conflict during the months leading up to the wedding. Generally, people can agree on the "right thing" even if it's not "their thing."

Second, etiquette eases the way for guests of both the wedding and all related parties. When there are set rules to follow, they won't worry about details such as how to RSVP, what to wear, whom to bring and what to give as a gift. Without these worries, the stage is set for everyone to direct their full attention to celebrating the couple at the center. Speaking of that couple, remember to consult them on (nearly) everything, at least at the beginning stages of whatever you are planning.

> *TO THE BRIDE AND GROOM—*
> *MAY THEY HAVE A LIFETIME OF LOVE*
> *AND AN ETERNITY OF HAPPINESS.*

HOW TO USE THIS BOOK

WORDS ARE THE FOCUS: just as bookworms wriggle below the radar in high school popularity contests, words often get lost in the flurry of flowers, cake fillings and table settings, but they are the most integral detail. When used incorrectly, they draw negative attention. When used correctly, they bespeak civility. When used eloquently, they are unforgettable.

Parents and attendants have concerns apart from those of the bride and groom, but their to-do lists are also overflowing: How do you word the official engagement announcement? How about the shower invitations? Who toasts at which party? And how does a person who's not accustomed to public speaking pull off a toast that sparkles with sentiment and wit? Chapters are organized by roles: Chapter 1 is for the parents, Chapter 2 for the maid of honor and bridal party and Chapter 3 for the best man and groomsmen. Chapter 4 tackles wedding toasts, and Chapter 5 is about postwedding instances that require the attention of parents and attendants. The quotes throughout the book are meant to serve as inspiration for your toast or even as part of the actual toast. You'll read in Chapter 4 that it's entirely acceptable to borrow another's words if you doubt that you're likely to come up with anything more poignant on your own. Jot down ideas for toasts, shower themes and everything else in the notes pages at the end. You never know when the perfect idea for a guest-book epigraph might pop into your head.

Chapter One

PARENTS OF THE BRIDE AND GROOM

In all of the excitement of learning that a son or daughter is engaged, it's easy to get ahead of yourself and begin thinking straightaway about china patterns and heirloom lace. Keep in mind that your first duty as the parents of the bride or groom is to receive your child's happy news with love and enthusiasm.

In fact, it's best not to mention the wedding day at all until the happy couple raises the topic themselves. While a proposal ventured and accepted does imply that a wedding will follow, the bride and groom should be given ample space to announce these plans in their own time. For now, your place is to express your best wishes on their engagement and welcome your son or daughter's betrothed into your family.

Once the wedding plans are broached, it's still wise to show restraint. Instead of rushing up to the attic to bring down your grandmother's gown, which you know

DISAPPROVING OF THE ENGAGEMENT

Although engagements are supposed to be happy events, there are times when a parent disapproves of a child's choice of a future spouse. If this unfortunate scenario occurs, there is a proper way to handle it. When the engagement is announced, stay calm. It's never a good idea to automatically object or show your disappointment. Any fears that you have should be addressed in an adult manner. Your worries may be unfounded and could be easily overcome with proper discussion—an abrupt objection could cause unnecessary damage to your relationship with your son or daughter.

will fit your future daughter-in-law perfectly, sit down for a conversation with the newlyweds-to-be. What is their vision? What is yours? No doubt everyone will have different ideas. An open-ended chat sets a genteel tone for a special occasion.

MEETING THE OTHER FUTURE IN-LAWS

TRADITIONALLY, THE GROOM'S PARENTS contact the bride's parents via handwritten note or a phone call after learning of the engagement, but today e-mail is also acceptable. If you opt to send a note, it should be gracious and welcoming. Try to initiate a get-together if the families live near one another. Sample wording:

Dear Michael and Kristin,

I wanted to write and let you know that John just told us the good news! Cheryl is such a lovely person, and we're extremely pleased and honored to welcome her into our family. We're happy to be gaining such a wonderful extended family and look forward to becoming better acquainted with you. Let's get together soon to celebrate this happy occasion.

Best wishes,
Heath and Iris

If the parents live far from one another, it's likely that they haven't met. In this instance, the note should be a bit more formal but still gracious and welcoming. It may not be possible to meet in person, but taking a weekend trip is a nice gesture, especially if the trip allows for visiting the bride- and groom-to-be and scouting rehearsal-dinner venues. Sample wording:

Dear Mr. and Mrs. Irving,

I wanted to write and let you know that John just told us the good news! Cheryl is such a lovely person, and we're extremely pleased and honored to welcome her into our family. We've heard so much about you, and we thank you for the kindness you've already shown to our son. We look forward to meeting you and becoming acquainted with your family. Hopefully we can plan a trip to meet before the wedding formally brings us together.

Best wishes,
Heath and Iris Preheim

If no gesture is made within ten days of the engagement by the groom's parents, it's fine for the bride's parents to take the initiative or for the couple to plan to bring their parents together. This meeting offers a great opportunity for a discussion confirming logistics such as wedding

> *Love is born with the pleasure*
> *of looking at each other,*
> *it is fed with the necessity*
> *of seeing each other,*
> *it is concluded with*
> *the impossibility of separation.*
> —*José Martí*

date and location as well as who's planning and hosting which of the many wedding-related parties. In many cases future in-laws may have already met, and the engagement provides an excuse for them to become even better acquainted. If so, the above rules still guide the get-together: the groom's parents should take the initiative.

ENGAGEMENT ANNOUNCEMENTS

HISTORICALLY, ANNOUNCEMENTS or "banns" were made to the general public in order to give people a chance to object to the proposed union. Nowadays, this broad announcement is simply meant to let others know about the marriage rather than to give them a say in whether or not it should occur. Because of this, it's very common to wait until the wedding to announce the news in a newspaper, alumni magazine, or any other publication. Some of the more superstitious consider announcing an engagement a potential jinx, especially if you haven't yet set a date. Some other reasons to wait:

- If your son or daughter is planning a long engagement. (Save yourself from running into people a year after the announcement has run and having to answer awkward questions about why the wedding hasn't yet occurred.)

- If your son or daughter is a widower or a divorcée, and former family members do not yet know of their plans. Or if they may be technically still married to someone else.

- If you'd like to include a picture from the wedding day.

If there is no reason to wait, one or both sets of parents may want to run a newspaper announcement in their

> *MAY YOU BOTH GROW OLD UPON ONE PILLOW.*
>
> —ARMENIAN

WELCOME TO THE FAMILY

Writing a note or calling your son or daughter's intended to welcome him or her into the family is a gracious gesture. Even if you've already communicated the sentiment in front of others, telling him or her one-on-one is more meaningful and is a great way to begin a cordial lifelong relationship.

respective hometown publications and perhaps in other places such as private-club or association newsletters. For announcements to run in high school or college alumni magazines, the bride and groom are in charge of submissions. For all announcements, inform the engaged couple so they're aware of the impending publication of the news. This will help ensure not only that they can start to expect correspondence from those who read the announcement, but also that they don't send duplicate announcements to the same publications.

To begin the submission process, call the editorial office at the publication and ask them about their guidelines, deadlines and, if applicable, fees. Some publications have a boilerplate form they will ask you to fill out. Others will ask for a write-up that is not to exceed a certain number of words. Usually an announcement includes the following information:

- Who's hosting the wedding

- Parents' names and places of residence

- Bride and groom's ages, career and education credentials, place of residence if it's different from those of the parents

- Wedding date, month or season ("A June wedding is planned," or "A fall wedding is planned.")

- Engagement photo (if they run photos)

GETTING APPROVAL

Remember, it's courteous not only to inform your son or daughter beforehand of all printed material you generate regarding their engagement and wedding but also to ask him or her to review the final draft. This includes everything from announcements to morning-after brunch invitations. It's for everyone's benefit. Your son or daughter will be more sensitive to details and to family situations and may pick up on a misspelling or a potential for toe trampling that completely passed you by.

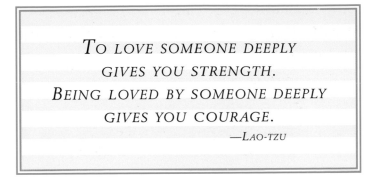

To love someone deeply
gives you strength.
Being loved by someone deeply
gives you courage.

—*Lao-tzu*

The more complex the family situation, the more the wording becomes like figuring out a complicated long-division problem. Here are some samples:

BRIDE'S PARENTS

Mr. and Mrs. Noah Fletcher of Saddle Brook, New Jersey, announce the engagement of their daughter, Kayla Noelle, to Matthew McGuire, son of Michael and Petra McGuire of Cherry Hill, New Jersey. Ms. Fletcher, a graduate of University of Pennsylvania Law School, is an associate at Whiteman, Jones & Kotter, a firm in Scarsdale, New York. Mr. McGuire graduated from St. John's University and is a professor at the City University of New York. A spring wedding is planned.

Single Parent

The engagement of Ms. Robin Margaret Altman, daughter of Mr. Duane Altman and the late Mrs. Gloria Altman, to Mr. George Brown, son of Barry and Caroline Brown of Wynewood, Pennsylvania, is announced by the bride's father. . .

Remarried Parent

Ms. Gloria Hillford and Mr. Kyle Hillford announce the engagement of Ms. Hillford's daughter, Ms. Jodi Elizabeth Banks, to Mr. Frank Bellows. . . . Ms. Banks is also the daughter of Mr. David Banks of Peoria, Illinois.

Bride and Groom

Ms. Nancy Rodgers, an independent graphic designer, is to be married to Mr. Christopher Bollman, an associate with Whiteman, Jones & Kotter. Ms. Rodgers is a daughter of the late Patsy and Abraham Rodgers of Saddle Brook, New Jersey. Mr. Bollman is the son of Gregory and Emily Bollman of Phoenix, Arizona. A spring wedding is planned.

When sending in an announcement to the local paper, be sure to include your daytime phone number just in case there are any questions regarding your submission.

You don't want to give the newspaper any reason not to run the announcement.

PRINTED ANNOUNCEMENTS

In addition to calling friends and family to herald the news, you may want to send formal announcements in the mail. Typically, these are sent by the host of the wedding, so the decision of who's hosting needs to be made before the announcements are printed. Also, sending formal announcements means making decisions about the size of the wedding and the guest list, since everyone who receives an announcement should also be invited to the wedding.

Many consider the save-the-date card that's sent by the bride and groom to double as an engagement announcement, but you may still wish to send your own formal cards. If so, the bride and groom should have some say in the choice of stationery and the wording. A straightforward notice on a simple ecru or ivory card sends an elegant message.

From the bride's parents:

MR. AND MRS. SEAN DUDGEON

ANNOUNCE THE ENGAGEMENT

OF THEIR DAUGHTER,

SHEILA CHRISTINE

TO

JOHN EDWARD BLOOMBERG

SON OF

MR. AND MRS. NOAH BLOOMBERG

From the groom's parents:

MR. AND MRS. NOAH BLOOMBERG

JOYFULLY ANNOUNCE THE ENGAGEMENT OF

SHEILA CHRISTINE, DAUGHTER OF

MR. AND MRS. SEAN DUDGEON

TO THEIR SON

MR. JOHN EDWARD BLOOMBERG

Expect plenty of phone calls and e-mails in response to the engagement announcements. Many will call simply to express their delight; others will be curious about the location and date of the wedding and even whether they can expect to play some role during the ceremony. If these details haven't yet been ironed out, simply tell the curious callers that you'll let them know as soon as there's a solid date and plan. Although you may be heavily involved in the planning and very much in the know, it's best to keep things quiet until the bride and groom have given you the green light. Make an exception only if the guest is a wedding VIP and has a specific conflict; for example, if he or she is in the middle of planning a trip around the same time as the wedding.

THE ENGAGEMENT PARTY

TRADITIONALLY, ENGAGEMENT PARTIES were thrown to announce the impending nuptials to the friends and family of the bride and groom. It would be the first event at which the bride would wear her engagement ring. Today, though that tradition is sometimes upheld through a surprise announcement, engagement parties are used more as a chance for friends and family of the bride and groom to get to know each other before the wedding.

> *LOVE DOES NOT CONSIST
> IN GAZING AT EACH OTHER,
> BUT IN LOOKING OUTWARD
> IN THE SAME DIRECTION.*
> —ANTOINE DE SAINT-EXUPERY

The engagement party is generally hosted by the bride's parents. The groom's parents may offer to help, or they may opt to throw an additional engagement party in their own town, but the bride's family should always have the option of throwing the first fête. The celebration is usually planned to occur one month to four months after the engagement.

WHO'S INVITED?

Keep in mind that all engagement party guests should also be invited to the wedding—another opportunity to compile that list early!

ENGAGEMENT PARTY INVITATIONS

The invitations do not need to align visually and textually with the wedding stationery. Instead, tone should be dictated by the tone of your party: Is it cocktails at a swanky bar or an intimate, sit-down banquet? Informal or formal or somewhere in between? Choose your invitations and wording accordingly.

Though the bride and groom will want to register a few weeks before the engagement party, this information should be spread by word-of-mouth, and never printed on the invitations.

Sample wording:

You are cordially invited
to attend an
engagement party
given in honor of
Melissa Kate
and
Gregory Pinter
on Friday the 15th of November
two thousand and seven
at seven o'clock in the evening.
The Racquet Club
215 South 16th Street,
Philadelphia

INTRODUCING THE FUTURE
MR. AND MRS. GREGORY PINTER
PLEASE JOIN US FOR
AN ENGAGEMENT PARTY
HONORING
MELISSA AND GREGORY.
FRIDAY, NOVEMBER 15TH
7:00 P.M.
THE UNIVERSITY CLUB
8 GLENBROOK DRIVE, BERNARDSVILLE
ROSE AND DAVID JANNEY

MELISSA AND GREGORY
ARE ENGAGED!
COME SHARE OUR JOY AT
AN ENGAGEMENT PARTY
FOR FAMILY AND FRIENDS.
FRIDAY, NOVEMBER 15
AT 7:00 P.M.
THE FAMISHED FROG
18 TOWN LANE, BEDFORD
PLEASE R.S.V.P. BY NOVEMBER 7TH
215-555-5555

THE RULE OF RECIPROCITY

When considering the guest list, the rule of reciprocity need not apply: you're not required to invite a friend who invited you to her daughter's wedding, especially if you're not hosting. While it's nice to do so, it's also understood that circumstances change and that the guest list accommodates several constituents and is often beyond your control.

ENGAGEMENT PARTY TOASTS

THE ENGAGEMENT PARTY is where the first official toast to the newly engaged couple is given. This toast is normally made by the father of the bride. Although most people know about a couple's engagement before this point, the father's toast is the official announcement. During this toast the father welcomes the groom into their family and wishes for the couple's ongoing happiness and the success of the marriage. Often the groom follows this with a toast of his own. These toasts generally start about two-thirds of the way through the affair.

Rehearsal Dinner

ONCE THE WEDDING DATE AND LOCATION are set, the groom's family should begin planning the rehearsal dinner. Even though it still seems far in the future, it's important to book a venue early. Rehearsal-dinner spaces are often as in demand as reception spaces, especially during peak wedding-season months.

Talk with the bride and groom to come up with a plan. They'll provide a guest list and have some idea of what type of event they want. If it's a destination wedding, the bride and groom can put the rehearsal-dinner hosts in touch with the on-site wedding planner to help choose a setting and make reservations.

WHO'S INVITED?

The wedding party, close family members and the officiant form the nucleus of the group. But if many guests and family members are traveling from out of town, or if the wedding is in a distant location, it's *de rigueur* to host a dinner for this much-larger group.

If that's impossible because of finances or venue, talk with your son and his fiancée. They may delegate one of their honor attendants to organize a group dinner so that out-of-town guests will have somewhere to sup and a chance to get to know one another before the reception.

Since the rehearsal dinner is hosted by the groom's parents and the wedding reception is hosted by the bride's parents, the invites should remain separate. About a month before the date, send an invitation with details denoting where and when.

Some sample wording:

PLEASE JOIN US

FOR THE REHEARSAL DINNER

FOR THE WEDDING OF NADINE AND JOSEPH

FRIDAY, OCTOBER 20 AT 7:30 P.M.

IMMEDIATELY FOLLOWING

THE WEDDING REHEARSAL

TAVERN ON THE SQUARE

55 EAST 67TH STREET, NEW YORK, NY

MR. AND MRS. JOHN CARDIGAN

REGRETS ONLY BY OCTOBER 7

212-555-5555

> *HERE'S TO THE BRIDE THAT IS TO BE,*
> *HERE'S TO THE GROOM SHE'LL WED,*
> *MAY ALL THEIR TROUBLES*
> *BE LIGHT AS BUBBLES*
> *OR THE FEATHERS THAT*
> *MAKE UP THEIR BED!*

PLACE CARDS AND TOASTS

The rehearsal dinner is the perfect opportunity for the wedding guests to get to know each other before the wedding. They all have something in common—the radiant couple at the center of the event—and so they should all get along famously. For larger gatherings, place cards and seating charts will be necessary. There should be some mingling and mixing of groups to encourage new acquaintances and reunite old friends. If you are leaning toward the idea of a singles' table, first ask the bride and groom if this is something their single friends will appreciate.

When dinner is served, there is a series of toasts, the first of which is given by the father of the groom or whomever is hosting the dinner. He welcomes everyone and thanks the bride's parents for hosting the upcoming reception. Then the best man takes the mike and toasts the bride and groom. Guests are encouraged to toast the couple during the rehearsal dinner so that the toasts are evenly divided and neither the rehearsal dinner nor the wedding is too heavy on toasts. Also, the rehearsal dinner is a less daunting place to deliver a toast for those who are shy about public speaking. The bride and groom will give the final toast, thanking the groom's parents for the lovely dinner and the bride's parents for the reception and everything else the two parental couples have contributed to the happy event.

SEND-OFF BRUNCH

USUALLY HOSTED BY THE BRIDE'S FAMILY, the farewell brunch the morning after the wedding is open to everyone who was invited to the rehearsal dinner and usually also includes out-of-town guests and even in-town guests who'd like a chance to wish the bride and groom well one more time.

Send out a separate mailing about a month before the wedding so that guests who are traveling can plan accordingly. Coordinate the brunch's start time to coincide with out-of-towners' checkout times, so that they're never stranded. A buffet brunch is best since everyone will have different travel plans and will need to arrive and leave at staggered times.

The card announcing the brunch might read like this:

PLEASE JOIN US FOR BRUNCH
SUNDAY, OCTOBER 22
TEN O'CLOCK IN THE MORNING
AMERICAN SEASONS
12 SOUTH ORANGE STREET
CHESTER, MASSACHUSETTS

REGRETS ONLY BY OCTOBER 12
MR. AND MRS. DONALD SCHUYLER
207-555-5555

FATHERS' DUTIES

MOST WEDDING-RELATED DUTIES traditionally fall to the mothers of the bride and groom; of course, the fathers are welcome to get involved, too. In some rare cases they become even more involved than their wives, but the more typical scenario is that of a father who's swept up and promptly tossed out (or perhaps has jumped out) of the wedding-planning tornado. But there are plenty of tasks to be accomplished by the fathers of the bride and groom. For example:

- Help come up with the budget.

- Help create the family's guest list.

- Draw maps and directions for the wedding invitations.

- Look over vendor contracts before they're signed.

- Work on a song list for the reception.

- Work on both his and his wife's rehearsal-dinner and reception toasts.

- Find options for readings for the ceremony.

- Come up with music choices for the father/daughter dance. Here are some popular choices:
  "Can You Feel the Love Tonight" (Elton John)
  "Daddy's Little Girl" (Al Martino)
  "Thank Heaven for Little Girls" (Maurice Chevalier from *Gigi* or Merle Haggard)
  "What a Wonderful World" (Louis Armstrong)
  "Daddy's Hands" (Holly Dunn)
  "If I Could" (Ray Charles)
  "Unforgettable" (Natalie Cole/Nat King Cole)

"Isn't She Lovely" (Stevie Wonder)

"Lean on Me" (Bill Withers)

"Lullaby" (Billy Joel)

"Just the Way You Are" (Billy Joel)

"My Funny Valentine" (Carly Simon)

"My Girl" (The Temptations)

"Have I Told You Lately" (Van Morrison)

"Sunrise, Sunset" (Zero Mostel from *Fiddler on
the Roof*)

"The Way You Look Tonight" (Frank Sinatra)

"Times of Your Life" (Paul Anka)

"Turn Around" (Harry Belafonte)

"You Are So Beautiful" (Joe Cocker)

"Whenever I See Your Smiling Face"
(James Taylor)

MOTHERS AND THE
BRIDAL SHOWER

THE MAID OF HONOR AND BRIDESMAIDS traditionally throw the shower, but others may want to get in
on the action; for example, close friends of the mother of
the bride who may have known the bride since she was a
baby. Or the mother of the groom may want to throw the
bride a shower in her part of the country to give her own

> NOW YOU ARE TWO PERSONS
> WITH ONE LIFE BEFORE YOU,
> GO NOW TO YOUR DWELLING TO ENTER
> INTO THE DAYS OF YOUR LIFE TOGETHER,
> AND MAY YOUR DAYS BE GOOD
> AND LONG UPON THE EARTH.
> —APACHE WEDDING BLESSING

friends and relatives a chance to shower her future daughter-in-law. (Before sending out invitations, the mother of the groom should talk to the bride-to-be about logistics and whether or not she can fit this trip into her busy schedule.)

There can be as many showers as there are willing hostesses, with some caveats: make sure the bride wants this many showers. If her schedule's already bursting at the seams, the better idea might be to combine forces and host a few large parties rather than many small ones. And make sure no toes are trampled. Consult with the maid of honor about her plans and plan for yours to happen after hers. (For more details on throwing a shower, see Chapter 2.)

The mother of the bride can take advantage of the shower to make a poignant toast to her daughter. Since this is one event she is surely not hostessing, she'll even have some downtime before the party to think about what she'd like to say to her daughter in the presence of this tight-knit group of women. Perhaps she'll share a funny anecdote about when she was a little girl playing Bride and Groom with her Barbies, and then she'll segue into how proud she is of the woman her daughter has become.

Something else for the bride's mother to commandeer at the shower is a "Words of Wisdom" journal or a blank journal whose first page she has filled with advice to her daughter on how to build a strong and happy marriage. Pass the book around during the shower so that the rest of the women can write their own words of wisdom.

MORE MOTHER-OF-THE-BRIDE DUTIES

THE MOTHER OF THE BRIDE used to run the show, but in modern times her level of involvement runs the gamut from guest to bride's assistant to hands-off hostess and all the way up to the customary role of director/producer. Where the mother of the bride falls

> *HERE'S TO THE BRIDE:*
> *MAY YOUR HOURS OF JOY*
> *BE AS NUMEROUS AS THE PETALS*
> *OF YOUR BRIDAL BOUQUET.*

within this continuum depends on the bride and groom. An older, established couple may decide to throw the wedding on their own. Regardless of all of this, the bride is still going to need plenty of help, and there are many ways for her mother to offer assistance. Here are some of her traditional duties:

- Compile in a timely fashion the names and addresses of family members and friends for the guest list.

- Offer to act as point person for wedding vendors, especially if the wedding is to be held in your hometown or region.

- Ask in-the-know friends for recommendations for exceptional sites and vendors.

- Research family traditions and heirlooms that the bride and groom may want to include in the ceremony and reception.

- Since the registry information should never be printed on an invitation or on any other wedding stationery, you share the duty of spreading the word about where your daughter and her fiancé are registered.

- Remind your husband to talk with your daughter about choosing their father/daughter dance song.

- Remind the bride often that she will be a beautiful bride, that you are extremely proud of her and that she has made an excellent selection for her life mate.

MANAGING RSVPS

If this duty is delegated to the mother of the bride, then the self-addressed, stamped envelopes inside the invitations will be addressed to her. She should remind her daughter to assign each guest a number and to write the numbers on the backs of the reply cards so that she knows who has replied even if the guest has illegible handwriting or has forgotten to sign his or her name.

Keep track of replies as they arrive (an electronic spreadsheet is an effective method) and manage those

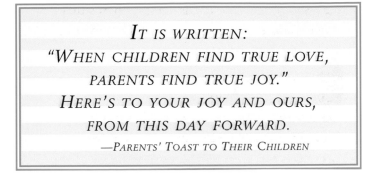

IT IS WRITTEN:
"WHEN CHILDREN FIND TRUE LOVE,
PARENTS FIND TRUE JOY."
HERE'S TO YOUR JOY AND OURS,
FROM THIS DAY FORWARD.
—*PARENTS' TOAST TO THEIR CHILDREN*

guests who, intentionally or not, stretch the boundaries of RSVP etiquette. For example:

- If someone replies for more guests than were invited, the mother of the bride needs to phone that person to let them know that unfortunately there is only room for the invited number. (She might soften the blow by assuring the person that she'll phone should another spot become available before the wedding.)

- If someone replies with children for a no-children wedding, she'll need to phone that person to break the news. If enough people insist on bringing children, she'll need to consult with her daughter about the possibility of hiring a babysitter or two for the evening.

- If people fail to respond to the RSVP by the stated date, she'll need to phone them to find out if they will be attending. If the person who didn't respond is on the groom's side, she'll inform her daughter so that her fiancé or his mother can make those calls.

- If the mother of the bride is also in charge of the guest list, she can also take the reply cards on which people have written personal messages and make them into a nice scrapbook for the engaged couple.

THE SEATING CHART

Assigned seating for the reception is a good idea; guests like to know where to sit, and this helps the caterer find the guests who've requested special meals. The mother of the bride usually assists the bride with the seating chart once the head count is set, usually about two weeks before the wedding date.

If the mother of the bride has been keeping track of RSVPs, she will be most familiar with who is coming and who is not. The bride and her mother need to sit down with the list of attendees and organize. The easiest way to do this is with an electronic spreadsheet because you can sort the information by any column desired using one centralized list.

> *AS YOU MAKE YOUR WAY*
> *THROUGH LIFE TOGETHER,*
> *HOLD FAST TO YOUR DREAMS*
> *AND EACH OTHER'S HANDS.*

If all the guests are already listed in a spreadsheet, simply add two columns to the existing sheet: one for "relationship to the bride and groom" and one for "table number." If they are not already in the spreadsheet, create a sheet with three columns, including the two listed above and the name of the guest.

- Categorize each guest as "high school friend of the bride," "high school friend of the groom," "college friend of the bride," "college friend of the groom," "work friend of the bride," "work friend of the groom," "bride's family," "groom's family," "friend of the bride's family," "friend of the groom's family" and so on. Re-sort the list so the categories are grouped together; this will help you visualize the tables.

- In general, seat those who know one another together. Don't fret if there are a few work

> *HERE'S TO HEALTH, PEACE*
> *AND PROSPERITY;*
> *MAY THE FLOWER OF LOVE*
> *NEVER BE NIPPED BY THE*
> *FROST OF DISAPPOINTMENT;*
> *NOR SHADOW OF GRIEF FALL*
> *AMONG A MEMBER OF THIS CIRCLE.*
> —*IRISH TOAST*

friends who don't fit at the work-friend table. There should be some mixing and mingling. The bride and groom will know who will get along with whom.

MOTHER-OF-THE-GROOM'S DUTIES

THE MOTHER OF THE GROOM can also be of great help to the busy, engaged couple. Here's how:

• Offer financial assistance to the groom as necessary.

- Compile names and addresses of family members and friends for the guest list, making certain not to ask to invite more than the allotted number of people.

- Offer to call unresponsive guests who are your own friends or family three to four weeks before the wedding to find out whether or not they'll be attending.

- Spread the word to your side of the family about where the bride and groom are registered.

- If the wedding is in your hometown or region, offer to help scout sites and vendors and, once contracts are signed, to serve as point person.

- Decide with your son on a song for your mother/son dance. Here are some popular choices:

  "Blessed" (Elton John)

  "Could I Have This Dance" (Anne Murray)

  "Close to You" (The Carpenters)

  "Have I Told You Lately" (Rod Stewart or Van Morrison)

  "Loves Me Like a Rock" (Paul Simon)

  "I Can See Clearly Now" (Johnny Nash)

  "I Wish You Love" (Gloria Lynne)

"In My Life" (The Beatles)

"Wind Beneath My Wings" (Bette Midler)

"Moon River" (Andy Williams)

"Stand by Me" (Ben E. King)

"Through the Years" (Kenny Rogers)

"Unforgettable" (Natalie Cole/Nat King Cole)

"What a Wonderful World" (Louis Armstrong)

"You Are the Sunshine of My Life" (Stevie
Wonder)

Some grooms leave this entirely up to their mom and some want input; ask your son what he'd prefer.

WHO WRITES THE CHECK?

TO THE GUESTS, the wedding will appear as if the event materialized effortlessly. But those who are behind the scenes know differently; they're the ones who deliberated over myriad choices and signed their names on dotted lines to authorize the existence of each and every gum-paste flower and Japanese paper lantern. Knowing which of the many accoutrements is your financial responsibility is part of being an exemplary attendant and/or family member. Here's a simple guide to the traditional breakdown of financiers:

> *HAPPY MARRIAGES BEGIN WHEN*
> *WE MARRY THE ONE WE LOVE*
> *AND THEY BLOSSOM WHEN*
> *WE LOVE THE ONE WE MARRIED.*
> —*SAM LEVENSON*

BRIDE AND FAMILY

- Engagement party

- Invitations, announcements and programs

- Bridesmaids' luncheon

- Rental fee for ceremony venue

- Reception

- Bride's gown and accessories (veil, etc.)

- Flowers for ceremony, reception, bouquets for bridesmaids and flower girls

- Groom's wedding band

- Transportation of bridal party to and from different venues on wedding day

- Wedding photography

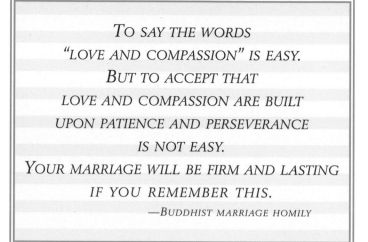

TO SAY THE WORDS
"LOVE AND COMPASSION" IS EASY.
BUT TO ACCEPT THAT
LOVE AND COMPASSION ARE BUILT
UPON PATIENCE AND PERSEVERANCE
IS NOT EASY.
YOUR MARRIAGE WILL BE FIRM AND LASTING
IF YOU REMEMBER THIS.
—BUDDHIST MARRIAGE HOMILY

GROOM AND FAMILY

- Whatever parties they choose to host in addition to the rehearsal dinner

- Marriage license

- Officiant's fee

- Groom's outfit

- Boutonnieres for groomsmen, bride's bouquet, corsages for mothers and grandmothers

- Bride's engagement ring and wedding band
- Honeymoon

MAID OF HONOR AND BRIDESMAIDS

- Their gowns
- Bridal shower
- Optional additional engagement parties or showers
- Bachelorette party

BEST MAN AND GROOMSMEN

- Their outfits
- Bachelor party

Chapter Two

THE MAID OF HONOR
AND BRIDESMAIDS

At the top of the list of attendants' duties are cohosting the bachelorette party and shower, keeping track of gifts given at the shower and at other prewedding parties and being prepared to give a toast at the rehearsal dinner and/or reception. Read between the lines of this list, and you'll see that the actual role of an attendant is to support the bride whenever she needs a hand and to bear witness to the events leading up to her very important day.

Not only do a bride's attendants stand solidly by the bride's side, but they also add significance and meaning to all of the main events with their presence and their words, both spoken and written. The paper trail begins when an attendant graciously accepts a bride's request to join her bridal party. Though not required, a handwritten note expressing happiness for her happiness and excitement over being an important part of her march toward the aisle is a beautiful gesture.

RSVP Etiquette

EVEN IF YOU THINK IT'S CLEAR that you're attending the wedding—you're a bridesmaid, after all—you do need to reply promptly upon receiving the wedding invitation. As an attendant, you should set an impeccable example and make the bride's life easy. Remember that being an attendant doesn't give you any special dispensation: you don't have the option, for example, of waiting until the day before the wedding to tell the host whether or not you want to bring a date.

If a reply card and self-addressed stamped envelope are provided, fill out the card as directed. If the invitation comes without a reply card but is stamped with the letters RSVP, you're required to write your own reply on your own stationery, mirroring the wording on the invitation.

> *MAY YOU BE POOR IN MISFORTUNE,*
> *RICH IN BLESSINGS,*
> *SLOW TO MAKE ENEMIES,*
> *QUICK TO MAKE FRIENDS.*
> *BUT RICH OR POOR, QUICK OR SLOW,*
> *MAY YOU KNOW NOTHING BUT*
> *HAPPINESS FROM THIS DAY FORWARD.*
> —*IRISH BLESSING*

You will do the same if the provided reply card is blank. Here's an example of how you might word your reply:

JASMINE FORTUNA AND JONATHAN DONBERRY

ACCEPT WITH PLEASURE

THE INVITATION OF

MR. AND MRS. KYLE LOGAN

FOR SATURDAY, THE 20TH OF OCTOBER

AT FIVE-THIRTY P.M.

BALLROOM AT THE BEN

(When replying with a guest, write out his or her full name so the reception host knows how to write your guest's place card.)

DECODING THE
WEDDING INVITATION

WEDDING INVITATIONS can be as inscrutable as the Rosetta Stone; until you've received more than a handful, the codes can seem more like cuneiform than English. However, as a member of the wedding party, you must be able to help with any questions guests may have.

DRESS CODE

As bridesmaid, your clothing will generally be dictated, however, you'll still need to be able to advise your date or other guests how to dress for the occasion. To interpret the dress code from the invitation, look to the bottom right-hand corner of the invite for a clue. Here's how it might read:

Black Tie: Evening dresses (short or long) for women; tuxedos for men.

Black Tie, Long Gown: Not common but found occasionally.

Black Tie Optional: Evening dresses (short or long) for women; tuxedos or dark suits for men.

> *AT THE TOUCH OF LOVE,*
> *EVERYONE BECOMES A POET.*
> —PLATO

Creative Tie: A dress other than black for women; a tuxedo or suit with a colorful twist (i.e. patterned cummerbund) for men.

TO BRING THE CHILDREN OR NOT?

Should the bride and groom have decided on a child-free affair, there's a good chance they've already begun to spread the word; they may even have asked for your help initiating some targeted word-of-mouth. If not, this decision will be explicit in the invitation: if the envelope is addressed only to the adults in the family, you can assume that the event is meant to be only for adults. Look to the RSVP card for another clue: if the names of the invitees are spelled out and only the names of adults appear, this is an indication that children are not invited. If the wedding hosts have decided not to invite children, it's your duty as a good guest not to question that decision, although you may ask whether child care will be available during the ceremony and reception.

The Bridal Shower

WHILE NOBODY CAN DETERMINE the exact origins of the bridal shower, it is believed to have originated centuries ago in the Netherlands when a young woman fell in love with a poor miller. They planned to marry, but her father disapproved and refused to hand over her dowry. The villagers and other friends of the couple came together and provided enough gifts to compensate for the withheld dowry, and the couple was able to marry.

Today the bridal shower is a much happier occasion. It serves as a chance not only to celebrate the upcoming marriage, but to shower the bride with presents and knowledge which will help her build a household. It also allows people from the groom's family to get to know the bride better before the big day. Ladies-only is still the most prevalent type of shower, and although Jack and Jill (coed) showers are gaining in popularity, there's something nice about the old-fashioned notion of the shower as an opportunity for several generations of women to

> *TAKE EACH OTHER*
> *FOR BETTER OR WORSE*
> *BUT NOT FOR GRANTED.*
> *—ARLENE DAHL*

share well-won wisdom about marriage, men, children and keeping house.

The maid of honor and her attendants cohost the shower anywhere from six months to a week before the wedding. Make sure to check with the bride on her availability since the final months leading up to the wedding can be packed with appointments and other obligations. Although the attendants are in charge of organizing and hosting the bridal shower, they should feel comfortable asking the bride's aunt(s) and/or sister(s) for some help—especially if a nearby relative has a big enough parlor for tea for twenty.

SHOWER INVITATIONS

Invite only those who will also be invited to the wedding, and be sure to consult the bride for a list of her close female friends and relatives to whom you may never have been introduced as well as women on the groom's guest list who should be included, such as the mother of the

> *WE CANNOT REALLY LOVE ANYBODY*
> *WITH WHOM WE NEVER LAUGH.*
> —*AGNES REPPLIER*

groom, sisters and other close female friends or relatives. The sky's the limit as far as style—choose a design that matches the tone (formal or informal) and theme. Invitations should be mailed at least four weeks in advance of the event and should include the following information:

- *Who's hosting?* Name(s) of hostess(es)

- *Who's the guest of honor?* Bride's full name (especially as she won't have the same last name as her hosts)

- *When and where?* Date, time and location, possibly including a map and directions for out-of-towners

- *How?* RSVP date and contact info (e-mail address and phone number for one point person). If possible, make it a cell number so that the chosen host is easy to reach should anyone need last-minute directions.

- *What should I bring?* If the shower has a theme (see themes on page 64), make this clear on the invitation. The stores at which the bride and groom are registered should never be printed on any wedding stationery, shower invite included. It's the job of the attendants and the couple's close family members to spread the word.

Some sample wording:

YOU ARE INVITED TO ATTEND A BRIDAL SHOWER
IN HONOR OF REBECCA STERN
SATURDAY, JUNE 10TH, AT FOUR O'CLOCK
THE TEA ROOM,
201 71ST STREET, NEW YORK, NY

PLEASE RSVP TO ALICIA STERN BY JUNE 1
203-555-5555
ASTERN@MYMAIL.COM

If the event has a theme, you can add that information before the RSVP line. Or, if the theme calls for a certain type of gift, you might insert a separate piece of paper that says something like, "For this around-the-clock shower, please bring a gift that relates to your assigned hour of 10 A.M."

SHOWER THEMES

Around the Clock: Each guest is assigned a time of day and is instructed to bring a gift that the bride might use during that particular hour (for example, a toaster or espresso maker at 10 A.M., a cuddly robe or silk peignoir at 10 P.M.)

Linen: The party is a basic shower, an afternoon luncheon for the ladies, but the guests are asked to stock the bride's linen closet.

Wine Tasting: Perfect for the oenophile. The shower's at a restaurant with a fabulous wine list or maybe at a vineyard; gifts are wine-related.

Kitchen: For the foodie, this theme is more about the gifts than the décor and content of the party.

Pick a Room, Any Room: You could throw a bedroom shower, a bathroom shower, a home-office shower, or a dining-room shower, depending on which room the bride-to-be most needs furnished or where she spends most of her time.

> *To the two secrets to*
> *a long-lasting happy marriage:*
> *Here's to a good sense of humor*
> *and a short memory!*

Stock the Bar: Probably a late-evening shower; gifts include glassware, barware and other entertainment accoutrements.

Around the World: Gifts from around the world or a group gift of a paid vacation or airline miles.

Flower Shower: For the inner florist, a flower-bedecked shower with flower- and garden-themed gifts.

Couples: Men are invited, and the shower is more likely a cocktail party or summer barbecue than the standard afternoon luncheon or tea party.

Shower Toasts

Ask people before the shower if they'd like to make toasts. This is a good time for a great-aunt or a second cousin to make a toast, since the closest friends and family will toast during the rehearsal dinner and wedding. That said, the mother of the bride may want to make a

GREAT GIFTS ON PAPER

Some of the best gifts don't come wrapped in a box:

- A gift certificate for a private session with a photographer.
- Tango lessons for two at a local dance school.
- A weekend at a nearby B&B either to unwind in the midst of wedding planning or to have something to look forward to post-wedding.
- Spa day gift certificate.
- A yearlong membership to a wine-, cheese- or fruit-of-the-month club.
- A yearlong subscription to a home magazine, if the newlyweds will be buying a new house.

toast at the shower, since, in the company of women and surrounded by her own good friends, she may feel it's an opportunity to articulate a special message.

TRACKING GIFTS

Before the shower, one bridesmaid should volunteer to keep track of gifts. As hostess, the maid-of-honor will have her hands full. The gift-tracking bridesmaid should come prepared with paper and a pen.

Whoever is keeping track of the gifts should write down who the gift is from and any details that will come in handy when the bride is writing thank-you notes. This could include everything from color and quantity to the expression of the bride when she opens the gift.

GUEST BOOKS

A guest book can double as a scrapbook. Employ some advance planning to help create a book that's a keepsake:

- A bridesmaid with an affinity for photography can rent or borrow a Polaroid camera or mini-printer to use with a digital camera to capture each guest on film. This enables you to insert the photos on-site into a blank scrapbook using photo corners or double-sided tape. Then you can ask guests to write a message to the bride on the page that features their photo.

- If a mini-printer or Polaroid camera is not readily available, bring a regular or digital camera. Also bring a blank book so the guests can write messages to the bride. Add the photos to the book once they're developed, along with candids and group shots, the shower invitation and messages from attendants.

> *TO KEEP YOUR MARRIAGE BRIMMING,*
> *WITH LOVE IN THE WEDDING CUP,*
> *WHENEVER YOU'RE WRONG, ADMIT IT;*
> *WHENEVER YOU'RE RIGHT, SHUT UP.*
> —OGDEN NASH

- Ask everyone to bring a photo of themselves with the bride. Encourage childhood friends and family members to bring old shots. After you put them in the book, the bride will have a "This is your life" album featuring all of her closest female friends and family members.

- Ask everyone to create a unique page of their own using a loose-leaf letter-size piece of paper and to bring it to the shower or mail it if they can't attend. Once at the shower, you'll put all of the pages together in a binder to produce a colorful, one-of-a-kind guest book. This way it's easy to include guests who can't make it.

Either limit the scrapbook to the shower or buy a larger volume in which you can memorialize everything leading up to the wedding: the bachelorette party, various spa days, dress fittings and anything else that might help the bride recall these happy, fleeting moments. Reveal the finished scrapbook a few weeks after the bride returns from her honeymoon. Arrange a gathering with the bridesmaids; the bride might be suffering from wedding withdrawal, and she'll welcome the chance to revisit these recent happy events.

BRIDESMAIDS' LUNCHEON

FROM A MONTH TO A FEW DAYS before the wedding, the bride invites the bridal party to a luncheon to thank them for all of their hard work and steadfast support. At this luncheon (or sometimes at the rehearsal dinner) the bride will give her bridesmaids and maid of honor a gift to show her appreciation. Often this gift has something to do with the wedding. For example, many brides present gifts of jewelry, which is to be worn during the wedding ceremony. Whatever these gifts are, accept them graciously and reply promptly with a handwritten thank-you note.

While there is no obligation for the bridesmaids to get the bride a gift at this function—they have after all purchased a number of gifts, their attire for the wedding and helped pay for the bachelorette party—it is sometimes done as a group gesture to give something sentimental rather than purely functional.

GIFT FOR THE BRIDE

The traditional bridesmaids' group gift for the bride was a sterling silver tray engraved with the bridesmaids' initials. Think about reviving the tradition; even the most modern brides will be able to make use of a classic silver tray.

THE BACHELORETTE PARTY

THOUGH THESE PARTIES tend to carry a colorful reputation, bachelorette fêtes come in many forms. Depending on the tastes and demeanor of the bride-to-be, a bachelorette party might consist of a long dinner at a fancy restaurant, a low-key spa day, a wine-tasting weekend, a long weekend at a beach house or even a few nights of gambling in Vegas (bachelors do not have a lock on that one).

Typically the bachelorette party happens after the bridal shower and closer to the wedding, from a month to a week before the event and often on the same night or weekend as the bachelor party. It's thrown by the bridesmaids with the maid of honor at the helm. No family members should be asked to cohost; this is strictly among the girls.

Moms and older relatives are best left off the guest list. The bride may not feel comfortable letting her hair down in the presence of her mother and future mother-in-law. The bride should be consulted on the guest list and should have the opportunity to sign off on the final list.

Since the bachelorette party is a less formal occasion, an e-mail invitation or invitations via telephone are fine. But should you feel inspired, a printed invitation always goes the distance when you're aiming to set a certain tone, and the bachelorette invitation begs for whimsy and creativity. You can really have fun with this one.

THE RECEIVING LINE

I F THE WEDDING IS TRADITIONAL, one of your duties as a member of the bridal party is to be a part of the receiving line after the ceremony. The purpose of this tradition is to give the guests the chance to congratulate the happy couple. It also gives the bride and groom an opportunity to greet each of the wedding guests personally and thank them for their attendance.

As a bridal attendant, your greetings to the guests should be short and pleasant, so the receiving line is constantly progressing. If someone tries to engage you in conversation, let them know that you will catch up with them later during the reception. Make sure you also keep an eye on the guests talking to the bride and groom. If you see that someone is chatting for an extended period of time, you can help out by gently urging an end to the conversation by politely presenting the next guest in line to the bride or groom.

CYBERCOMMUNICATION

WHEN IS IT OKAY and when is it not okay for attendants to use e-mail? There are some instances that are particularly well suited to the instant, informal mode of communication. Others need to adhere to tradition. How do you decide which falls under which umbrella? Here are some guidelines:

- Appropriate uses of e-mail
  - For the maid of honor to introduce herself to the bridesmaids.
  - For the long-distance attendants who may not know their fellow attendants to get to know each other before the wedding.
  - For invited guests to RSVP for prewedding parties.
  - For the attendants to discuss the logistics of the prewedding parties.

> *WHEN THE ONE MAN*
> *LOVES THE ONE WOMAN*
> *AND THE ONE WOMAN*
> *LOVES THE ONE MAN,*
> *THE VERY ANGELS DESERT HEAVEN*
> *AND SIT IN*
> *THAT HOUSE AND SING FOR JOY.*
> —*BRAHMA SUTRA*

- For informal invitations, such as those to the bachelorette party or to dress fittings with the bride.

- For sharing pictures and garnering feedback on visuals of bridesmaids' dresses, group gifts and shower venues.

• Inappropriate uses of e-mail

  - To RSVP for the wedding.

  - To invite people to the bridal shower.

  - To write anything that you wouldn't want to end up in the wrong in-box, such as a comment about someone else in the wedding party.

Chapter Three

THE BEST MAN AND GROOMSMEN

The groomsmen's duties are less well defined than those of the female attendants. Among their major tasks are planning the bachelor party; acting as charming, de facto hosts during each prewedding event; and decorating the "getaway" vehicle. In addition, the best man acts as toastmaster at the rehearsal dinner and reception.

RSVP Etiquette

Although it is evident that you will be attending the wedding—you're in it, after all—it is still necessary to RSVP promptly after receiving the wedding invitation. As a member of the wedding party, you not only want to set a good example, you want to do everything you can to make the groom's life easier. There is no special dispensation just because you are a part of the wedding. For example, you shouldn't wait until the day before the event to tell the host that you would like to bring a date.

If a reply card and self-addressed stamped envelope are provided, fill out the card as directed. If the invitation comes without a reply card but is stamped with the letters RSVP, you're required to write your own reply on your own stationary, mirroring the wording on the invitation.

You will do the same if the provided reply card is blank. Here's an example of how you might word your reply:

Jonathan Donberry and Jasmine Fortuna

accept with pleasure

the invitation of

Mr. and Mrs. Kyle Logan

for Saturday, the 20th of October

at five-thirty p.m.

Ballroom at the Ben

> *THERE IS NOTHING MORE*
> *LIVELY IN LIFE THAN*
> *THE UNION OF TWO PEOPLE*
> *WHOSE LOVE FOR*
> *ONE ANOTHER HAS GROWN*
> *THROUGH THE YEARS*
> *FROM THE SMALL ACORN OF PASSION*
> *INTO A GREAT ROOTED TREE.*
> —*VITA SACKVILLE-WEST*

(When replying with a guest, write out his or her full name so the reception host knows how to write your guest's place card.)

DECODING THE WEDDING INVITATION

IF YOU HAVEN'T HAD a great deal of experience with wedding invitations, they can sometimes be a bit difficult to interpret. However, as a member of the wedding party, you must be able to help with any questions guests may have. Here are a couple things you should be able to tell from the invitation.

DRESS CODE

Look to the bottom right-hand corner of the invite for a clue as to how to dress for the occasion. Here's how it might read and how you should interpret the words:

Black Tie: Evening dresses (short or long) for women; tuxedos for men.

Black Tie, Long Gown: Not common but found occasionally.

Black Tie Optional: Evening dresses (short or long) for women; tuxedos or dark suits for men.

Creative Tie: A dress other than black for women; a tuxedo or suit with a colorful twist (i.e. patterned cummerbund) for men.

TO BRING THE CHILDREN OR NOT?

Should the bride and groom have decided on a child-free affair, there's a good chance they've already begun to spread the word; they may even have asked for your help initiating some targeted word of mouth. If not, this decision will be explicit in the invitation: if the envelope is addressed only to the adults in the family, you can assume that the event is meant to be only for adults. Look to the RSVP card for another clue: if the names of the invitees are spelled out and only the names of the adults appear, this is an indication that children are not invited. If the

> *THERE IS NOTHING NOBLER OR*
> *MORE ADMIRABLE THAN WHEN*
> *TWO PEOPLE WHO SEE EYE TO EYE*
> *KEEP HOUSE AS MAN AND WIFE,*
> *CONFOUNDING THEIR ENEMIES*
> *AND DELIGHTING THEIR FRIENDS.*
> —HOMER, THE ODYSSEY

wedding hosts have decided not to invite children, it's your duty as a good guest not to question that decision, although you may ask whether child care will be available during the ceremony and reception.

BACHELOR PARTIES

BACHELOR PARTIES DATE BACK to fifth-century Sparta, when soldiers feasted and toasted each other on the eve of a wedding. In later incarnations, the men threw their glasses to the ground once they had made their toasts so the glass would never be used for any less worthy purpose. This custom of smashing remains a relic, but the bachelor party is still very much alive and kicking.

Depending on the personality of the groom-to-be, the bachelor party activities can range from a calm night out with a few friends to a wild adventure. The one thing that all bachelor parties have in common is the fact that the group is doing something above and beyond what they would normally do. For example, you could have a calm evening out at an expensive or trendy restaurant where you normally wouldn't go. Or, if the groom likes adventure sports, you could take a trip to go white-water rafting. The bachelor party serves as a chance for the groom-to-be to make the most of his final days as a single man. It's a rite of passage from bachelorhood to the more adult life of a married man.

Though various movies would have you think that the bachelor party convenes the night before the wedding, this is actually a horrific proposition and one that won't serve the groom or his attendants well in the end. Besides,

LOVE IS NOT FINDING SOMEONE TO LIVE WITH, IT'S FINDING SOMEONE YOU CAN'T LIVE WITHOUT.
—RAFAEL ORTIZ

the eve of the wedding is reserved for the rehearsal dinner. The bachelor party should be scheduled, like the bachelorette party, about a month to a week before the wedding. It's practical to coordinate with the bridesmaids while planning the party so that you choose the same night or weekend as the bachelorette party. This way, neither mate is pining for the other, as each is kept very busy by his or her pals.

BACHELOR PARTY INVITATIONS

OLDER RELATIVES AND THE FATHER of the bride should not be invited to the bachelor party. It's up to the groom to decide whether or not he would like his own father to attend. Remember, the bachelor party is the time to share the kinds of stories that may not be appropriate for a more genteel audience. The groom should be consulted on the guest list and should have the opportunity to sign off on the final list.

Because the bachelor party is an informal occasion, invitations by phone or e-mail are acceptable, but feel free to send a physical invitation if you feel inspired. If this is a destination party, be sure to include all the pertinent travel and lodging information and a schedule of all planned events.

> *To the Bride and Groom:*
> *May all their troubles*
> *be little ones.*

The Getaway Car

DECORATING THE GETAWAY CAR is the province of the best man and groomsmen. First, find out what time the couple is likely to drive off. Ask the wedding planner. If there's no wedding planner, ask the hostess or the maid of honor. Make sure the car is bedecked well before the couple's estimated time of departure.

Purchase the materials in advance, and make sure they're safe, i.e., no wrecking the car's paint job. This means no spray paint, electrical tape or whipped cream (sugar damages paint). If the car is a dark color, write on the body with an ordinary bar of soap or a water-soluble marker. Use the same on windows. Wedding specialty shops and Web sites sell magnetic signs and "clings," vinyl decals that peel off easily. It's also possible to glue custom-made signs or enlarged photos onto magnetic sheets from a craft store, but first make sure the car's body panels are metal, not plastic. Or hang a charming hand-decorated cardboard sign over the trunk using ribbons.

Here are some ideas for what to write:

Just Married

Newlyweds

Together Forever

We Tied the Knot

Josh and Jessica [the bride and groom's names]—
    Just Married

To complete the look, tie helium-filled balloons and bunches of flowers to the door handles, luggage rack and hood ornament. (Use sturdy blooms such as mums, carnations and roses.) Wrap ribbons around the antenna and the four corners of the luggage rack so they'll flutter in the wind when the car is in motion. Create a garland, or order one from the florist, to drape over the car's grill or bumper. Finally, the classic: attach plastic bottles and old shoes to dangle from the  car's bumper. Leave off the tin cans; they make dangerous sparks.

OTHER BEST-MAN DUTIES

- Sign the marriage license.

- Give the officiant his payment following the ceremony. This payment should have been given to you by the groom or his family prior to the wedding.

- Take care of tips for wedding-day vendors such as band, caterer and bartender.

- Collect gift envelopes and hold them for safe-keeping until the bride and groom return from their honeymoon.

- Hold the rings until the groom needs them during the ceremony.

CYBERCOMMUNICATION

WHEN IS IT OKAY and when is it not okay to use e-mail? There are some instances that are particularly well-suited to the instant, informal mode of communication. Others need to retain an air of tradition. How do you decide which falls under which umbrella? Here are some guidelines:

- Appropriate uses of e-mail

  - For the best man to introduce himself to the groomsmen.

  - For the long-distance groomsmen who may not know their fellow attendants to get to know each other before the wedding.

  - For sending bachelor party invites.

  - For invited guests to RSVP for the bachelor party.

  - For discussing the logistics of the bachelor party and the details of decorating the getaway car.

  - For sharing pictures and garnering feedback on links to bachelor party venues and group gifts.

- Inappropriate uses of e-mail

  - To RSVP for the wedding.

  - To write anything that you wouldn't want to end up in the wrong in box, such as a comment about someone else in the wedding party.

Chapter Four

WEDDING TOASTS

Though the origins of the toast cannot be unequivocally determined, it is believed that the term came from the old tradition of putting a piece of spiced toast into wine to improve the flavor. Since this wine and spiced toast combination was commonly used to honor someone and bestow good tidings, a metaphor arose that compared the honoree to the piece of toast—the honoree adds flavor to a situation just as the toast does to the wine. Though the tradition of adding toast to wine has passed, the use of the term remains strong.

A good toast should be short and easy to say, and it should be full of sentiment and wit. Not an easy combination! The best man plays a significant role during the reception's toasts; as toastmaster, he's responsible for arranging the schedule beforehand. He should ask the bride and groom about their expectations regarding the toasting portion of the evening: are they hoping for a free-for-all or would they prefer that just the attendants and family members toast? Iron out these details and make sure that all who are scheduled to honor the happy couple know where they fall in the toasting order so that they're prepared when their time arrives.

GENERAL ETIQUETTE

- If you're making a toast but you don't drink alcohol, ask the server for some other beverage. Make sure you have a glass of something.

- When you make a toast, stand up and walk to the microphone so that everyone can hear what you're saying. Look around the room, but make eye contact with the bride and groom during most of the toast.

- Keep your toast short; two to three minutes is plenty. If you find that you have so much to say

> *EVERYTHING COMES TO US*
> *FROM OTHERS;*
> *TO BE IS TO BELONG TO SOMEONE.*
> —*JEAN-PAUL SARTRE*

that your toast is turning into a speech, check with the best man to see if this is all right. He may or may not have too many people on the toasting schedule to allow a full-fledged speech.

- At a formal wedding, address the crowd as "ladies and gentlemen" or "honored guests," and other guests by their proper titles should you refer to them.

- The bride and groom will stand up and raise their glasses to you once you've finished toasting them.

- The best man will take the mike from you and then introduce the next person on the toasting schedule.

> *LET ANNIVERSARIES COME*
> *AND LET ANNIVERSARIES GO—*
> *BUT MAY YOUR HAPPINESS*
> *CONTINUE FOREVER.*
>
> —*ANONYMOUS*

WHO AND WHEN?

- Toasts usually begin after cocktails, once everyone has been seated for the meal and has been served a drink.

- The best man gets everyone's attention by taking the microphone and introducing himself: "Good evening, my name is John Smith. I'm the best man. I'd like to propose a toast to Nancy and Ward."

The maid of honor can serve as comaster, or she can simply make a toast after the best man. One or both should be given the responsibility of figuring out the toast order so they can keep the evening running smoothly and make sure no one feels slighted for not getting a turn at the mike.

- The groom responds to the best man and toasts his new wife and also offers thanks and appreciation to his parents, whether they are hosting the reception or not. These days, it's becoming common for the bride to toast her new husband and her guests. (Traditionally, the bride toasts her husband and in-laws at the rehearsal dinner— the reception is the groom's domain.)

- Though there is a traditional toasting structure, nothing is written in stone; if the best man or the father of the bride happens to feel anxious about public speaking, he should be relieved of these duties.

- The toasts can continue, or they can be interspersed throughout the meal, between courses— a good option when there are a lot of toasts.

- Parents might want to toast, especially if they're hosting the reception, and so too might other relatives and friends. The groom's parents typically toast at the rehearsal dinner, which can also be a good occasion for other family members and friends to say a few words. People might feel more comfortable sharing their sentiments in this more relaxed and casual setting, and this helps keep the number of toasts down during the wedding, freeing up time for eating and dancing.

- If there are still more people who'd like to toast but who didn't get a chance, there's always the postwedding brunch. The bride and groom will figure out before the wedding who's toasting at which occasion. If a parade of friends and family approaches the bride and groom about toasting, they may decide to break things up by assigning some to the rehearsal dinner, some to the reception and some to the postwedding brunch. If this is the case, they may ask anyone who isn't an honor attendant or family member to toast at the rehearsal dinner and brunch.

- If someone who, for whatever reason, isn't part of the evening's agenda, and would like to toast, as toastmaster the best man is responsible for letting this person know that it's not possible. The best man might say: "I'm sorry, but we've reached maximum capacity with the toasts. As it is, there's hardly time for the guests to enjoy their dinner."

- If you think someone might want to make a toast, you should ask, and tell him or her to let the maid of honor or best man know before the reception so that person is factored into the toasting schedule.

- At a Jewish wedding, the father of the bride begins the meal at the reception by saying a blessing over a loaf of challah bread. The blessing is sometimes preceded by a toastlike speech. At Roman Catholic and other Christian weddings, a blessing is said before the meal is served.

CLANGING THE GONG

UNFORTUNATELY TOASTS DON'T ALWAYS come off as planned. For whatever reason, a guest or family member might forget that there are others waiting on deck and chatter on past the unsaid, but generally understood three-minute maximum. It is up to the best man, the toastmaster, to politely interrupt. Remember that

MAY YOU BE MERRY AND LACK NOTHING.
—WILLIAM SHAKESPEARE

this is a joyous occasion, and any cutting off of speeches must be done with lightness and finesse. Here are some tips for how to remain respectful during this extremely difficult task:

- The toastmaster should first indicate to the person toasting that his or her time is up by walking over to the toaster and standing expectantly nearby. This may be enough of a hint in itself.

- If that doesn't do the trick, the best man should try and make eye contact with the speaker, using that moment to point to his watch or to make a "wrap it up" gesture.

- If the speaker continues to be oblivious to his faux pas, the best man has no choice but to walk up to the speaker, simultaneously engaging the audience in a round of applause by beginning to clap. Once the toast maker can no longer be heard, he will have no choice but to surrender the microphone.

---

*HERE'S TO THE GROOM
WITH BRIDE SO FAIR,
AND HERE'S TO THE BRIDE
WITH GROOM SO RARE!*

- Once the best man recovers the microphone, he should not draw any further attention to the person who needed to be interrupted. Instead, he should proceed as if everything has gone smoothly by thanking that person for his heart-felt words and cueing the next toast maker.

Although the general rule is to keep speeches short, remember that there are certain situations where you should be more lenient and let the speech continue. Ask yourself whether the bride and groom would prefer that you not interrupt the toast maker. After all, the toasts are meant for the happy couple, and if you know that the toast maker is, for example, an elderly relative who is especially dear to the bride, you may choose not to interrupt.

Also remember that there are reasons other than length of the speech to interrupt. If the toast maker is being inappropriate or offensive, you have a right to cut the speech short. But remember to be respectful even in this scenario. You and the bride and groom may want to establish some kind of signal that will tell you whether or not you should step in.

What to Say

ON'T TRY AND STYLE YOURSELF into a modern-day Shakespeare. Just talk as if you're addressing your friends (without any vulgarities or inappropriate anecdotes, of course). Keep it chatty, funny, poignant and short. And heed Mark Twain, who quipped, "It takes three weeks to prepare a good impromptu speech." Prepare well in advance.

If you're not a natural toast maker, it helps to break the toast down into three parts: the introduction, the tribute and the toast. During the introduction, announce your name and your connection to the bride and groom. Relate it to the occasion. Be specific, such as "Good evening. I've been a friend of the groom's since we met our freshman year at Yale. It was a time in his life when he was more interested in sports than girls. I honestly wondered if he'd ever look away from the game long enough to find a woman, much less convince one to marry him. I certainly never imagined he'd end up with someone as wonderful—and so obviously superior to him in intelligence, beauty and wit—as Dahlia."

Next comes the tribute, when you say something complimentary about the bride and groom. You might share a personal anecdote about the first time you saw them together or when you realized she was the right

CONQUERING YOUR FEAR
OF PUBLIC SPEAKING

- Practice, practice, practice. While you're practicing, notice where you pause naturally and indicate these pauses in your notes to remind yourself to breathe while you're at the mike.

- Find out beforehand exactly where your friends and family are sitting so that you can make eye contact with your support system as you deliver your toast. Their kind eyes will bolster your confidence.

- Remember that this is an easy crowd; they're at a wonderful party, and they're basking in the glow of enduring love. They want to love your toast. They want to laugh at your jokes.

- Though a few sips of wine may help, too much will definitely hurt. Don't drink in order to feel more relaxed for your toast. Alcohol is a depressant, and overdoing it may depress your ability to speak clearly, not to mention impairing your common sense.

woman for him. Ask yourself the following questions to spark some ideas for content:

- How long have you known them?

- How did you meet them?

- Do you have any funny memories involving one or both of them?

- Do you remember the first time your friend told you about the man or woman who'd become his or her future spouse?

- When did you first think to yourself that they were good together?

- Do you remember talking about this with one of your mutual friends?

- What are five words that come to mind when you think about the groom? The bride? How are they similar? How are they different?

- What are your wishes for their future together?

If you're still stumped, you might consider asking the bride or groom—whichever one you know best—what you should say and what it is they love about their mate.

During the tribute, talk about both the bride and groom even if you only know one of them well. And

> *MATRIMONY—THE HIGH SEAS*
> *FOR WHICH NO COMPASS*
> *HAS YET BEEN INVENTED.*
> —HEINRICH HEINE

leave the private jokes out of the toast; your sentiments should be clear to everyone in the room, even great aunts and third cousins.

Last, you will raise your glass while you propose a toast to the couple.

Here are some more ideas for the toast's content:

- Consider using someone else's words to start off the toast: begin with a quote that begs further discussion. For example: "Someone once said, 'Everyone admits that love is wonderful and necessary, yet no one agrees on just what it is.' Well, I can't presume to provide you with a definition, but I do know that I see it when Louis looks at Denise. . . ."

- Here's another idea that might spark some poignant material: ask a child what marriage and love is, and use his or her thoughts to start off the "tribute" part of your toast.

- There might be a traditional toast that older family members have used at previous weddings. Ask around; it would be nice to continue this family tradition.

- Always end on a high note, with your best wishes for the couple's future.

What Not to Say

JUST AS THERE ARE COMMON TOPICS to include in a speech—how you know the couple, how wonderful the bride and groom are, etc.—there are many topics you should avoid.

The first thing to keep in mind when you're writing your speech is the audience. Remember, this speech may be for the bride and groom, but it's being said in front of everyone from the groom's six-year-old nephew to the bride's great aunt Hester. The stories you relay must be appropriate for all of the ears in the room. It's best not to recount stories from the groom's frat party days or the bride's hilariously out-of-character trip to Vegas.

Bawdy stories aren't the only things to avoid—there are also many hot-button issues. Follow the rule of thumb for casual conversation: don't talk about politics or religion. While you should avoid politics entirely, religion can be included if the wedding is a religious event.

> KEEP LOVE IN YOUR HEART.
> A LIFE WITHOUT IT IS LIKE A SUNLESS
> GARDEN WHEN THE FLOWERS ARE DEAD.
> THE CONSCIOUSNESS OF LOVING
> AND BEING LOVED BRINGS A WARMTH
> AND RICHNESS TO LIFE THAT
> NOTHING ELSE CAN BRING.
> —OSCAR WILDE

However, it must be incorporated in the right way, such as with a quick prayer or blessing for the couple rather than proselytizing or trying to convert the audience.

Another thing to keep in mind is that not everyone will be able to attend the wedding. In some cases—such as a faraway, but dear, friend who was unable to make the trip—it's fine to mention their absence. If family members or intimate friends are deceased, it may be okay—and even welcome—to mention them, but never do so without consulting the bride and groom first. If the bride and groom don't mind the reference, be sure to make it short, properly reverent and positive. Mention something along the lines of how happy the deceased family member would be for the couple rather than a negative com-

AWKWARD WORDING

Some best friends share more than just clothes, and it's not entirely uncommon to have a set of close friends who have dated the same individual. Your relationship may not have succeeded, but if those two have found happiness, and you've maintained friendships with both, then you are a perfect person to give a toast.

It's fine to give your toast hefty doses of humor. It is, after all, a strange and interesting story that will give a little extra kick to the traditional "how they met" tale related in most toasts. Be certain, though, to mix in a heaping of tact. A little discretion can go a long way.

ment, like how there will always be something missing from the union due to the lost relative. In the case of an estranged but living family member, silence may, in fact, be golden.

Other sensitive subjects to avoid include past relationships of the bride or groom, the cost of the wedding, negative stories, and any kind of confidential information.

Remember also that the speech is in honor of the bride and groom. It should help the audience know the couple through your eyes—to see them as you do. While you'll have to talk a bit about your personal experiences to accomplish this, your focus should stay on the bride and groom.

WRITING THE TOAST

START WITH A ROUGH DRAFT: spill your thoughts onto a piece of paper or onto your computer without worrying about grammar, spelling or structure. Go back afterward and begin to hone and polish so that the toast fits into the three-part structure: introduction, tribute and toast.

Read the toast aloud to yourself. Does it sound stilted? Since people use more formal language when they write than when they speak, you will likely need to make some changes so you feel comfortable uttering the words. When you're ready, read the toast aloud to a friend for feedback on clarity, suitability and tone (is it as funny as you think it is?). You may need to explain some backstory or polish your delivery by emphasizing one sentence over another. All of this will iron itself out as you continue to practice the toast.

HOW TO BE A GOOD GUEST DURING A TOAST

Remain seated.

Listen intently. No whispering to your companion.

Laugh when you're supposed to laugh.

No editorializing. If you think you have something to add, it's best to keep it to yourself.

Have a glass filled with anything from champagne to club soda at the ready.

During the toasting portion of the toast, raise that glass and take a sip. Don't drain the glass of liquid.

(Don't practice it in front of too many people; you don't want the whole wedding party to know what you're going to say.)

DELIVERING THE TOAST

IF YOU ANTICIPATE coming down with a case of stage fright, write the entire toast in large letters on a piece of paper. If you think you'll be all right, just write the major points on an index card. Either way, you don't want to be reading from a piece of paper as if you're a grade-schooler being asked to read aloud from a text. Having just the major points in front of you will prevent that.

Some more pointers:

- Don't eat the microphone. You'll sound best when your mouth is about three inches away from the mike.

- Speak more slowly than you would during the course of a normal conversation.

- Be energetic and speak with animation: speed up to show excitement; slow down and pause for dramatic effect; gesture while you're talking; smile while you recount a funny anecdote.

- Make eye contact with the bride and groom, especially at the end, when you raise your glass, but during the rest of the toast make sure to look around the room. You're toasting the couple, but

MAY YOUR MARRIAGE BE MODERN ENOUGH TO SURVIVE THE TIMES, AND OLD-FASHIONED ENOUGH TO LAST FOREVER!

you're addressing all of the guests; make everyone feel included.

- Even if you can't memorize your entire toast, try and memorize the final sentences so that you can end on a strong note. Slow down and raise your voice to signal that you're coming to the end. Then make eye contact with the bride and groom and raise your glass as you complete the toast.

WORDS OF OTHERS

There are plenty of places to look for inspiration: old journals, letters and photos of your younger days with your altar-approaching friend. Other places to look are favorite novels, poems, movies, songs and even books of famous quotes. You might find that your feelings are best expressed by someone else's words. Quoting someone else is a great way to begin the "tribute" section or express the "toast" portion.

To weave the words of someone else into your toast, simply say something like, "As Shakespeare said," or "In the words of George Eliot…" Peppered throughout this book are a number of words from famous scribes who had a way with words. Look for inspiration in these scattered quotes and in those that follow:

> ### LET'S DRINK TO LOVE,
> ### WHICH IS NOTHING—
> ### UNLESS IT'S DIVIDED BY TWO.

What greater thing is there
for two human souls
than to feel that they are joined…
to strengthen each other…
to be at one with each other
in silent unspeakable memories.
—*George Eliot*

One word frees us of all
The weight and pain of life:
That word is love.
—*Sophocles*

You will find as you look back upon your life
that the moments when you have truly lived
are the moments when you have done things
in the spirit of love.
—*Henry Drummond*

Chains do not hold a marriage together.
It is threads, hundreds of tiny threads,
Which sew people together through the years.
—Simone Signoret

A great marriage is not when
the 'perfect couple' comes together.
It is when an imperfect couple
learns to enjoy their differences.
—Dave Meurer, "Daze of Our Wives"

Marriage is like paying an endless visit
in your worse clothes.
—John Boynton Priestley

A good marriage is one which
allows for change and growth
in the individuals and
in the way they express their love.
—Pearl Buck

Come live with me, and be my love,
And we will some new pleasures prove
Of golden sands, and crystal brooks,
With silken lines, and silver hooks.
—John Donne, "The Bait"

> MAY YOUR MARRIAGE
> BE LIKE A MIGHTY SHIP,
> ALWAYS HOLDING
> A TRUE AND STEADY COURSE,
> WEATHERING ROUGH SEAS WITH
> STRENGTH AND COURAGE,
> AND SAILING CALM WATERS
> WITH STYLE AND GRACE.

*A happy marriage is
the union of two forgivers.*
—*Ruth Bell Graham*

*The supreme happiness in life
is the conviction that we are loved—
loved for ourselves, or rather,
loved in spite of ourselves.*
—*Victor Hugo*

*Often the difference between
a successful marriage and a mediocre one
consists of leaving about
three or four things a day unsaid.*
—*Harlan Miller*

The moment you have in your heart
this extraordinary thing called love
and feel the depth, the delight, the ecstasy of it,
you will discover that for you the world is transformed.
　　　　　　　—J. Krishnamurti

A good marriage is like a casserole,
only those responsible for it
really know what goes in it.
　　　　　　　—Anonymous

The beginning of love is to
let those we love be perfectly themselves,
and not to twist them to fit our own image.
Otherwise we love only the
reflection of ourselves we find in them.
　　　　　　　—Thomas Merton

My true-love hath my heart, and I have his,
By just exchange, one for the other given:
I hold his dear, and mine he cannot miss,
There never was a better bargain driven.
　　　　　　　—Sir Philip Sidney, Song from Arcadia

When love speaks, the voice of all the gods
Make heaven drowsy with the harmony.
　　　　　　　—William Shakespeare

> ### HERE'S TO THE GROOM,
> ### A MAN WHO'S KEPT HIS HEAD
> ### EVEN THOUGH HE LOST HIS HEART.

Love must be as much a light as a flame.
— *Henry David Thoreau*

"Marriage": this I call the will
that moves two to create the one
which is more than those who created it.
— *Friedrich Nietzsche*

Success in marriage does not come
merely through finding the right mate,
but through being the right mate.
—*Barnett Brickner*

Our marriage works because we each carry clubs
of equal weight and size.
—*Paul Newman*

There is only one happiness in life,
to love and be loved.
—*George Sand*

Marriage is a great institution,
But I'm not ready for an institution.
                    —Mae West

A sound marriage is not based
on complete frankness;
it is based on a sensible reticence
                    —Morris L. Ernst

The sum which two married people owe to one
another defies calculation. It is an infinite debt, which
can only be discharged through all eternity.
                    —Johann Wolfgang von Goethe

It comes as a great surprise to younger people that a
husband and wife must work at marriage all the years
of their life.

                    —Dr. May E. Markewich

Marriage requires the giving
and keeping of confidences,
the sharing of thoughts and feelings,
unfailing respect and understanding,
and a frank and gentle communication.
                    —Richard L. Evans

> *MAY THOSE WHO ENTER*
> *THE ROSY PATHS OF MATRIMONY*
> *NEVER MEET WITH THORNS.*

The people who enjoy marriage are those who first have learned to live life itself. You can't create intimacy without identity.
> *— Richard Rohr*

My most brilliant achievement was my ability to be able to persuade my wife to marry me.
> *—Sir Winston Churchill*

Chapter Five

AFTER THE WEDDING

Finally! Time to relax. The wedding went off beautifully, and everyone is content, if a little tired, the next morning. Chances are the hosts and the bride and groom did not have a chance to wish everyone farewell at the end of the evening. The morning-after brunch, usually hosted by the bride's family, is a great opportunity to spend some more time with friends and relatives before everyone goes their separate ways. After the bride and groom have set off on their honeymoon, family and friends can choose to extend the experience in several ways.

> *MAY YOUR MARRIAGE*
> *BE LIKE A FINE WINE,*
> *GETTING BETTER AND BETTER*
> *WITH AGE.*

GIFT CARDS

YOU HAVE A YEAR from the wedding date to find the perfect gift for the bride and groom. Often, the perfect gift can be found on the registry. They're likely to have received all of the place settings except for one or all of their barware save for the ice bucket and port glasses. Purchasing the items to complete these sets is an excellent idea.

Now that you've chosen your gift, what should you say on your card? Think about what you want to express: congratulations are certainly in order. You will also want to personalize your words. Instead of a brief and generic "congratulations," you might write something like this:

Dear Neil and Rebecca,

Joel and I couldn't be happier for you. We knew from the moment Rebecca called the day after your first date that you were meant for each other, and, as always, we were right! Congratulations on finding your match. We wish you many years of love, health, happiness.

Much love,

Nancy and Joel

Or you may want to reference the gift. For example, if you purchased Champagne flutes:

Dear Katelyn and Chris,

We look forward to toasting your health and happiness for many years to come. Congratulations! We're so pleased for you.

All the best,

Tara and Frank

POSTWEDDING BRIDAL PARTY EXTRAS

EVEN AFTER THE LAST GUEST has gone home, the bride and groom (now husband and wife) are still

SAYING THANK YOU

Once they return from their honeymoon, the bride and groom will be busy writing thank-you notes. It's a nice gesture for attendants and family members to write their own notes:

- To the bride and groom thanking them for their own gifts and for having included them in the wedding.

- To the host and hostess of both the rehearsal dinner and reception for throwing such wonderful parties.

burdened with details. There are several ways members of the bridal party can continue to help:

- Take responsibility for collecting and keeping the special mementos safe until the bride returns from the honeymoon. This includes the cake topper, the top tier of the cake, stationery keepsakes (a menu card, place cards, programs) and the guest book.

- Before the couple leaves for their honeymoon, gift the bride with a honeymoon kit. Include a blank travel journal, a great beach book, a specialty travel guide that focuses on the food, architecture or art that they'll find at their destination. Chances are they haven't had time to find these extras.

And to cushion their return to reality:

- Write a "welcome home" card to greet them when they return. Leave it at their door or, if you have their house keys, inside their home along with a basket of treats.

- Collect your digital photos in an online album complete with captions, and e-mail the link to the bride and groom, the rest of the wedding party and to other guests and family members.

- Plan a post honeymoon get-together with the rest of the attendants to look at the scrapbook you started assembling before the wedding.

MARRIAGE IS A FRIENDSHIP RECOGNIZED BY THE POLICE.
—ROBERT LOUIS STEVENSON

NOTES

May your voyage through life
be as happy and as free
As the dancing waves
on the deep blue sea.

_____

_____

_____

_____

_____

_____

_____

_____

_____

_____

_____

_____

_____

_____

_____

_____

Love is not a matter of counting the years,
it is making the years count. Love is the
master key that opens the gates of happiness.

—OLIVER WENDELL HOLMES

When the roaring flames of your love have burned down to embers, may you find you've married your best friend.

_____

_____

_____

_____

_____

_____

_____

_____

_____

_____

_____

_____

_____

_____

_____

_____

_____

_____

_____

A successful marriage requires falling in love many times, always with the same person.

—MIGNON MCLAUGHLIN

_____

_____

_____

_____

_____

_____

_____

_____

_____

_____

_____

_____

_____

_____

_____

_____

_____

_____

There is a single magic,
a single power, a single salvation,
and a single happiness,
and that is called loving.

—HERMAN HESSE

_____

_____

_____

_____

_____

_____

_____

_____

_____

_____

_____

_____

_____

_____

_____

_____

_____

Remember always: arrows pierce the body,
but harsh words pierce the soul.

—SPANISH PROVERB

May your joys be as deep as the ocean and your misfortune as light as its foam.

Honor, riches, marriage-blessing,
Love continuance, and increasing,
Hourly joys be still upon you!
Juno sings her blessings on you

—SHAKESPEARE, THE TEMPEST, ACT IV

There is no surprise more magical than the surprise of being loved. It is God's finger on man's shoulder. —CHARLES MORGAN

INDEX